REVELATION

STUDY GUIDE

Revelation
Study Guide

J. J. Como

BVB

Bold Vision Books
P. O. Box 2011
Friendswood, Texas 77549

ISBN NO. 9780692438763

Published in the United States of America.

Bold Vision Books
PO Box 2011
Friendswood, Texas 77549

Cover Photo by Ricardo Reitmeyer

Interior by kae Creative Solutions

Dedication

It is my pleasure to dedicate and honor my husband Tony for these pages in which we labored together to finalize. Thank you for your encouragement and computer skills.

Love and blessings,
~~J. J. Como

Table of Contents

Table of Charts

Introduction

If you are interested in end time study, you know there are numerous books, charts, pamphlets, and movies on the subject. Each one gives views, scenarios, and then postulates what possibly could happen in the end of days.

So then, why write another book on this seemingly diverse and endless subject? I believe a fresh look at the book of Revelation is needed. So much has been written and stated, so it seems very complicated. Many are willing to take any opinion of these matters. I challenge you to wipe the slate clean of preconceptions and search with me to discover what the book of the Revelation actually says.

I encourage you to meditate and ponder with me. Let's ask God to show us the truths as we take the journey through these words. Let's ask Him to help us see what isn't true. Let's enjoy contemplating and understanding the Living Word of the King of Glory.

Oh, how I love a good mystery. The last book of the Bible, the Revelation of Jesus Christ, is a marvelous mystery, which unveils the glory of our Lord Jesus Christ. Join me as we fit all the puzzle pieces and clues together. When we are done, we will display an accurate and proper picture of the One who is coming to rule and reign. He will have the keys of authority over death and Hades. He is the King of kings, the Lord of lords, and the King of Glory.

Our template for the investigation will be the twenty-seventh book of the New Testament because this manuscript by the Apostle John gives us the most information concerning Jesus Christ's unveiling. Through John's writings, we will investigate His marvelous mystery.

Many think that the book of Revelation is far too difficult to understand, but may I encourage you; for if we read and hear with understanding, then heed the things written therein, Jesus promises a blessing.

> Blessed is he who reads and those who hear the words of this prophecy,
> and keep those things which are written in it; for the time is near
> (Revelation 1:3 NKJV).

If we study and know the book of Revelation:

1. We will not be tossed to and fro, here and there in doctrine when tumultuous events begin to happen on the earth.
2. We will be enabled to persevere in the Lord until the end, whether by death or life or the catching away of the church to be with the Lord.
3. We will have insight and understanding about the things occurring on earth in order to bring more people into the Kingdom of God, thus avoiding the wrath of God.
4. We will be able to answer questions from those who fear the afflictions to come on the earth, because these things must take place to usher in the ruling Kingdom of God.
5. We will warn, with conviction and compassion, unbelievers about the wrath to come.
6. We will know without a doubt that the Lord and Savior, Jesus, is coming back soon in all His majesty and glory.

We must be ready for the soon coming of the Lord Jesus Christ. Father God is clear in the first verse of the Revelation that He wants his bondservants to see and know what must shortly take place.

> The Revelation of Jesus Christ, which God gave Him to show His bondservants, the things which must soon take place; and He sent and communicated it by His angel to His bondservant John (Revelation 1:1 NASB).

What God desires His bondservants to be shown, I desire to see. So together let us look at the clues, signs, evidences, and puzzle pieces so we may see a clear and correct picture as portrayed in the Revelation of Jesus the Christ.

The commentary *Who is this King of Glory?* is unlike others you may have read. To know God and His Word in a deep way, we must do more than merely read Scripture and study what someone else has to say about it. I believe too many of us read the commentaries instead of the Word. It is my hope to see what the Scripture actually says about these end times. I have tried to approach the events in the book of Revelation without preconceived ideas. I did not start with a notion or theory about eschatology—the study of end times. I have not predetermined or defined any time periods, places, or ideas.

Instructions

Together, we will read and accept the words as they are written. We will make lists of what the verses actually say instead of what we think they mean. We will let the Scripture guide us to a conclusion. The method used to achieve the conclusions is derived from an inductive way of studying the Word of God. The meaning of inductive is to "reason from particular facts to come to a general conclusion."

As you work your way through this study guide, answer the questions with the facts and insights that Scripture gives instead of remembering what you've heard somewhere or sometime. Using the exactness of Scripture will help us come to conclusions that are true and right.

Along with the inspired Bible, our Teacher the Holy Spirit, leads us into all truth and reveals the things of God to us. Then, understanding is achieved. The Bible becomes its own commentary. After fully observing what the Scripture says, we will then search out other Scriptures in order to discover what the whole counsel of the Word of God reveals. Scripture never contradicts Scripture.

Revelation 1:19 NASB divides John's manuscript into three parts:

> Write the things which you have seen, and the things which are, and the things which will take place after these things.

1. The things which John has seen (chapter 1).

2. The things which are (chapter 2-3).

3. The things which shall take place after these things (chapters 4-22).

THE REVELATION OF JESUS CHRIST
AN OUTLINE

I.   Introduction (1: 1-8)

II.   Jesus Commissions John to Write (1: 9-20)

III.   MESSAGES TO THE SEVEN CHURCHES
    A.   Ephesus (2:1-7)
    B.   Smyrna (2:8-11)
    C.   Pergamum (2:12-17)
    D.   Thyatira (2:18-29)
    E.   Sardis (3:1-6)
    F.   Philadelphia (3:7-3)

IV.   THE THRONE ROOM IN HEAVEN
    A.   One Sitting on the Throne (4:1-10)
    B.   Seven-Sealed Scroll (5:1-5)
    C.   Lamb Slain (5: 6-14)

V.   THE SEVEN SEALS
    A.   SEAL ONE: White Horse (6:1-2)
    B.   SEAL TWO: Red Horse (6:3-4)
    C.   SEAL THREE: Black Horse (6:5-6)
    D.   SEAL FOUR : Ashen Horse (6:7-8)
    E.   SEAL FIVE : Souls Under the Altar (6:9-11)
    F.   SEAL SIX : Great Earthquake (6:12-17)

IX.   MARRIAGE OF THE LAMB (19:7-9)

X.   COMING OF THE LORD (19:11-21)

XI.   THE THOUSAND YEAR REIGN (20:1-6)

XII.   SATAN'S DESTRUCTION (20:7-10)

XIII.   GREAT WHITE THRONE JUDGMENT (20:11-15)

XIV.   NEW HEAVEN, NEW EARTH, NEW JERUSALEM (21:1-22: 5)

XV.   FINAL EXHORTATION OF JESUS (22: 6-21)

Session One
The Revelation to the Bondservants
Revelation Chapter 1

Read Revelation chapter 1 in your Bible.

Answer the following questions from the text.

Who wrote the book?

To whom was the book written?

How did John receive the Revelation?

What was the flow of the information?

What is the promise to the bondservant who reads, hears, and heeds Revelation?

Who is revealed?

What three things was John told to write?

List what you see in chapter 1 concerning:

God-

Jesus-

Holy Spirit-

John-

Bondservant-

List the mystery of the golden lampstands and the stars.

Lampstands-

Stars-

Session Two
The Churches in Asia
Revelation Chapters 2-3

Read Revelation 2:1-7 concerning the church at Ephesus.

> Using the Churches: Overcomers chart on page 23, list what the church at Ephesus was to overcome, how the church was to overcome, and the result of overcoming.

How is "first love" described?

Look up the following Scriptures and from each passage note in the space below what love is to look like.

Deuteronomy 30:15-20

Mark 12:28-34

1 Corinthians 13:1-13

Acts 2:41-47

The Churches: Overcomers

Churches	Overcome What	Overcome How	Overcoming Result
Ephesus			
Smyrna			
Pergamum			
Thyatira			
Sardis			
Philadelphia			
Laodicea			

Does your life line up with these actions? What steps can you take to begin living in this kind of love?

Read Revelation 2:8-11 concerning the church of Smyrna.
Using the Churches: Overcomers chart (Page 23) list what the church at Smyrna was to overcome, how the church was to overcome, and the result of overcoming.

The Smyrna church was known as the suffering church.

Read Revelation 2:12-17 concerning the church at Pergamum.
Using the Churches: Overcomers chart (Page 23), list what the church at Pergamum was to overcome, how the church was to overcome, and the result of overcoming.

What is the teaching of Balaam? Look up the following verses to help you answer:
Numbers 25:1-8

Revelation 2:14

Read Revelation 2:18-29 concerning the church at Thyatira.
Using the Churches: Overcomers chart list what the church at Thyatira was to overcome, how the church was to overcome, and the result of overcoming.

What is the teaching of Jezebel, the false prophetess of Thyatira?
See Revelation 2:20.

Read Revelation 3:1-6 concerning the church at Sardis.
Using the Churches: Overcomers chart (Page 23), list what the church at Sardis was to overcome, how the church was to overcome, and the result of overcoming.

What are the "white garments" referred to in Revelation 3:4-5? (See also Revelation 7:14 and 19:8.)

Read Revelation 3:7-13 concerning the church at Philadelphia.
Using the Churches: Overcomers chart (Page 23), list what the church at Philadelphia was to overcome, how the church was to overcome, and the result of overcoming.

What do you think "have kept My word" in Revelation 3:8, 10 means?

What is different about the way the Lord Jesus addresses this church compared to what he said to the other churches?

Read Revelation 3:14-22 concerning the church at Laodicea.

> Using the Churches: Overcomers chart (Page 23), list what the church at Laodicea was to overcome, how the church was to overcome, and the result of overcoming.

> What is different about the way the Lord Jesus addresses this church compared to how he spoke to the other churches?

> What is the condition of the church at Laodicea?

On the Churches: Overcomers chart (Page 23), review the list in the column of the Overcoming Result.

Session Three
The Heavenly Throne Room
Revelation Chapters 4-6

Read Revelation 4-5.

Where are the events taking place?

List what you learn in the verses concerning the One sitting on the throne, the Lamb, the Spirit, the living creatures, the elders, and the angels. Remember to only list the descriptions and facts from the verses.

One sitting on the throne-

Lamb-

Spirit-

Living creatures-

Elders-

Angels-

Read Revelation 6.

Using the Seals, Trumpets, and Bowls chart on the next page, make a list of what occurs for each seal as it is broken.

Seals, Trumpets, Bowls

	Seals	Trumpets	Bowls
1st			
2nd			
3rd			
4th			
5th			
6th			
7th			

Session Four
The 144,000 and the Great Multitude
Revelation Chapter 7

Read Revelation 7:1-8.

Who is sealed or marked in this passage?

When are they sealed?

How are they described?

What does the seal indicate?

Who do they belong to?

Where were they located when they were sealed? In heaven or on earth?

Read Revelation 7:9-17.

What group is addressed in this passage?

What are they declaring?

Where are they located?

What have they come out of?

What are they doing?

How are they described?

What are they promised?

Session Five
The Blown Trumpets
Revelation Chapters 8-9

Read Revelation 8.

Using the Seals, Trumpets, and Bowls chart (Page 29), list facts about seal 7.

List facts about the Trumpets 1-4 on the Seals, Trumpets and Bowls chart (Page 29).

What is the warning given in Revelation 8:13?

Read Revelation 9.

List the facts about Trumpets 5-6 on the Seals, Trumpets, and Bowls chart (Page 29).

What group of people is spared from Trumpet 5?

How long is Trumpet 5?

What is the warning given of Revelation 9:12?

How many of mankind is killed in Trumpet 6?

How large is the army of Trumpet 6?

What is the attitude of those left alive?

Session Six
The Strong Angel Announcement
Revelation Chapters 10-12

Read Revelation 10.

What is in the hand of the strong angel?

Look up Ezekiel 2:8-10 and 3:4, 6 for the identity of the little book (or scroll).

What will be finished at the sounding of the seventh trumpet?

What is the meaning of "the mystery of God"? (Look up Ephesians 3:4, 6 to help answer the question.)

What did the angel tell John to do with the "little book"?

Read Revelation 11: 1-14.

List below what is learned concerning the two witnesses.

Who causes the demise of the two witnesses?

Where do the events pertaining to the two witnesses fall in the sequence of the trumpet soundings?

Add these events to your Seals, Trumpets, and Bowls chart (Page 29).

Read Revelation 11:15-19.

On the Seals, Trumpets, and Bowls chart (Page 29), list what occurs with the sounding of the seventh trumpet.

Read Revelation 12.

What is learned concerning the persons in chapter 12?

Sign of the Woman-

Sign of the Dragon-

Session Seven
The Beasts and
The Angel Proclamations
Revelation Chapters 13-14

Read Revelation 13.

What do you learn from chapter 13 concerning the two beasts?

The Beast-

The Other Beast-

Read Daniel 7:2-8, 17, 19-27.

Do you see any similarities to the beasts of Daniel 7 and Revelation 13:2?

Read Revelation 14:1-5.

Who is this passage speaking of?

Where are they located?

How are they described?

Whom had they not been defiled by?

Read Revelation 14:6-20.

List what each angel is proclaiming.

1.

2.

3.

4.

5.

6.

Session Eight
The Bowls of God's Wrath
Revelation Chapters 15-16

Read Revelation 15.

How are the plagues of the seven angels described?

List what is learned concerning these who had been victorious.

Where are the events of Revelation 15 taking place?

Briefly list what is happening there.

Read Revelation 16.

List the events of the bowls on the Seals, Trumpets, and Bowls chart (Page 29).

Review the Seals, Trumpets, and Bowls chart (Page 29) and answer the question.

What do you observe as to the severity between the seals, the trumpets, and the bowls?

Considering the time phrases in Revelation, how do the events line up? Do they have an order, such as sequential, chronological, or any other observations?

Session Nine
Babylon, the Great Harlot
Revelation Chapters 17-18

Read Revelation 17.

List on the Babylon the Great Harlot chart (below) all the facts concerning Babylon in chapter 17.

Babylon the Great Harlot

Judgment of Babylon	Destruction of Babylon
Revelation 17	Revelation 18

Observe Revelation 17:7-13.

Explain what you think is meant in verse 8, "the beast… was, and is not, and is about to come"?

Who is in wonder at the beast?

What are the seven heads / seven mountains identified as?

What are the ten horns identified as?

When do the ten horns get their authority?

Who overcomes the beast with his ten horns?

Who has ultimate authority over these kings?

Read Revelation 18.

List on the Babylon the Great Harlot chart on page 41 all that is learned concerning the destruction of Babylon in chapter 18.

According to verse 3, who is associated with the mystery Babylon?

Who are "My people" spoken of in verses 4-6?

Who is the one who judges Babylon?

According to verse 24, whose blood is found in the city of Babylon?

Compare Revelation 17:6 with Revelation 18:24.

Session Ten
The Coming of the Lord Jesus
Revelation Chapters 19-20

Read Revelation 19:1-9.

What group is praising God in this passage?

Where are they located?

How is the great multitude described?

Compare the great multitude of Revelation 7:9-17 and Revelation 19:1-9.

Are they the same group?

What is the group ready for and why?

Read Revelation 19:11-21.

How is the Lord described?

What has the Lord come to do?

What is the result of the great supper of God?

Compare with Revelation 14:19-20 and Revelation 16:14.

Who makes war with the Lord?

What happens with each of them?

Read Revelation 20.

What happens to the dragon? For how long?

Who are included in the first resurrection?

How are they described?

What will they do with Jesus Christ?

What happens after the 1000 year rule of Christ Jesus?

Who is involved?

How does it end? For how long?

What happens to the dead?

Where does the judgment take place?

How are they judged?

Where are the dead, death and Hades sent?

Who is not involved in this judgment?

Session Eleven
The New Jerusalem
Revelation Chapters 21-22

Read Revelation 21.

Who is in the holy city, New Jerusalem?

How did the people get there to inherit these things?

Who will not be there?

List everything concerning the bride, the wife of the Lamb.

Bride-

Who becomes the temple in the New Jerusalem?

What is no longer needed for light there?

What will not be found in the city?

Read Revelation 22.

What tree is found in the city?

How is it described?

What relationship is between God, the Lamb and the bondservants?

What are the promises associated with Jesus' stating "I am coming quickly"?

What are the warnings associated with the book of Revelation?

www.ingramcontent.com/pod-product-compliance
Lightning Source LLC
Chambersburg PA
CBHW081527040426
42447CB00013B/3364